THIS LAND CALLED AMERICA: GEORGIA

CREATIVE EDUCATION

Published by Creative Education
P.O. Box 227, Mankato, Minnesota 56002
Creative Education is an imprint of The Creative Company
www.thecreativecompany.us

Book and cover design by Blue Design (www.bluedes.com)
Art direction by Rita Marshall
Printed in the United States of America

Photographs by Corbis (Bettmann, Tom Brakefield, Burstein Collection,
Lynda Richardson, John Van Hasselt), Getty Images (Altrendo Nature,
Clarence Sinclair Bull/John Kobal Foundation, Alfred Eisenstaedt/
Time & Life Pictures, Peter Essick/Aurora, FPG, Paul Harris, Imagno,
SATORU IMAI/A.collection, Kean Collection, Ken Krakow, Francis
Miller//Time Life Pictures, MPI, James Randklev, Don Allen Sparks,
Stock Montage, Randy Wells)

Library of Congress Cataloging-in-Publication Data
Shofner, Shawndra.
Georgia / by Shawndra Shofner.
p. cm. — (This land called America)
Includes bibliographical references and index.
ISBN 978-1-58341-635-8
1. Georgia—Juvenile literature. I. Title. II. Series.
F286.3.S56 2008
975.8—dc22   2007005684

First Edition
9 8 7 6 5 4 3 2 1

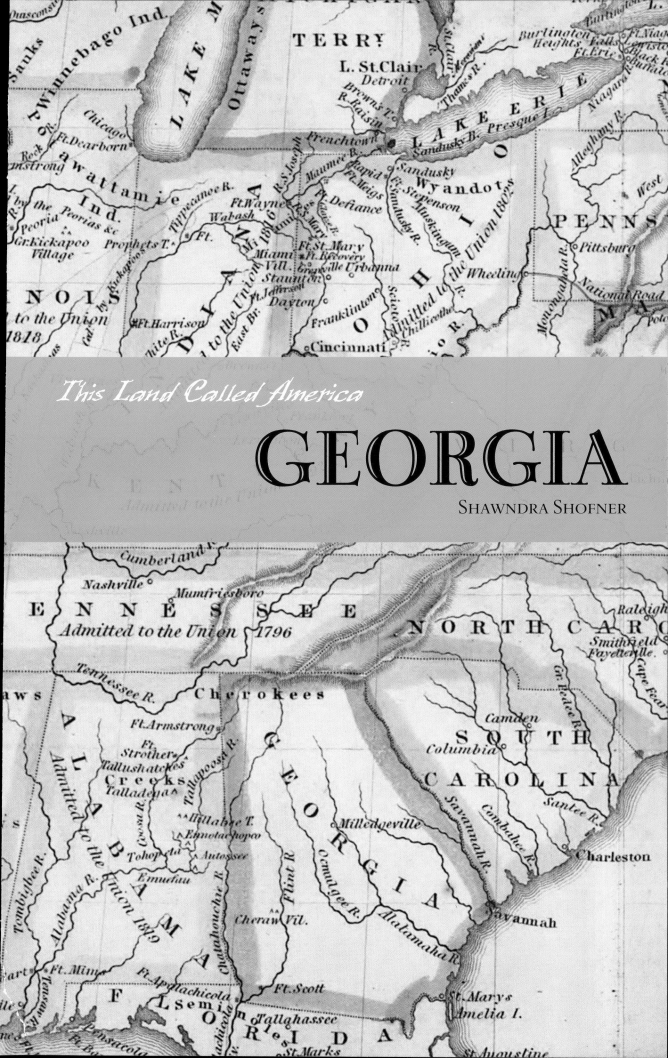

This Land Called America

GEORGIA

Shawndra Shofner

Georgia

SHAWNDRA SHOFNER

MORNING FOG RISES OVER TEA-COLORED RIVERS. TWO PEOPLE IN A CANOE PADDLE BETWEEN FLOATING ISLANDS CALLED HAMMOCKS. STARTLED ALLIGATORS SLIP QUIETLY INTO THE WATER. SPANISH MOSS HANGS FROM CYPRESS TREE BRANCHES. THE ROTTEN SCENT OF GREENBRIAR BUSH FLOWERS FILLS THE AIR. GOLDEN SILK SPIDERS MEND THEIR WEBS. SUNDEW PLANTS CATCH GNATS ON THEIR STICKY LEAVES. FAR AWAY, A SANDHILL CRANE TRUMPETS. THESE ARE SOME OF THE SIGHTS, SOUNDS, AND SMELLS OF GEORGIA'S OKEFENOKEE SWAMP. IT IS THE LARGEST SWAMP IN NORTH AMERICA, AND IT LOOKS MUCH THE SAME TODAY AS IT DID WHEN AMERICAN INDIANS FIRST CALLED THIS AREA OF SOUTHEAST GEORGIA HOME.

YEAR

1540 Spaniard Hernando de Soto explores Georgia, looking for gold.

EVENT

The 13th Colony

SPANISH EXPLORER HERNANDO DE SOTO WAS THE FIRST EUROPEAN TO VISIT GEORGIA. HE AND 600 MEN TRAVELED THROUGH THE LAND IN 1540. ONLY AMERICAN INDIAN PEOPLE FROM THE CREEK AND CHEROKEE TRIBES LIVED THERE THEN. THEIR ANCESTORS WERE THE MISSISSIPPI MOUND BUILDERS. THESE EARLY PEOPLE SHAPED THE EARTH INTO LARGE MOUNDS. THEY BUILT TEMPLES AND HOMES ON AND NEAR THEM.

Hernando de Soto

When the Spanish, led by Hernando de Soto (left), first explored North America, they sometimes came into conflict with American Indians (opposite).

During the 1600s, Europeans settled in 12 colonies along the Atlantic coast of North America. In 1732, England's King George II sent General James Oglethorpe to found a 13th colony. Oglethorpe landed at Yamacraw Bluff near Savannah. He met Mary Musgrove, a half-Creek, half-English woman. She owned a trading post and could speak the Indian language. She helped Oglethorpe make a treaty with Chief Tomochichi. The chief signed over lands to white settlers. Oglethorpe named the new colony Georgia after the king. The first settlers made their homes in Savannah.

YEAR
1733 English general James Oglethorpe founds Yamacraw Bluff (present-day Savannah) on the Savannah River.
EVENT

State bird: brown thrasher

England ruled the 13 colonies. The people who lived in the colonies could not make their own laws. They had to pay taxes to England, too. In 1775, the colonists rebelled against England, starting the Revolutionary War. Representatives from the 13 colonies signed the Declaration of Independence in 1776. Lyman Hall, George Walton, and Button Gwinnett signed the document for Georgia.

In 1778, English troops captured Savannah. Four years later, General "Mad" Anthony Wayne forced the English out. The Revolutionary War ended in 1783, and the United States won its freedom. Georgia became the fourth state on January 2, 1788, with former Revolutionary War army lieutenant colonel George Handley as its governor.

Eli Whitney moved from Connecticut to Georgia to become a teacher after graduating from college in 1792.

Georgian Eli Whitney invented the cotton gin in 1793. His first hand-cranked machine separated as much cotton from its sticky seeds in an hour as one slave could do in an entire day. Soon, Georgia farmers led the country in cotton production. By 1860, the state's population had passed 1 million, about 460,000 of whom were slaves who worked on cotton plantations, or big farms.

Whitney did not profit from the cotton gin (below), since others soon figured out how to make their own.

After Abraham Lincoln became president in 1861, Southern states were afraid of losing the right to own slaves. Eleven states, including Georgia, left the Union. They formed the Confederate States of America. In 1861, the Confederate and Union states began fighting in the American Civil War. A Confederate army won a battle at Georgia's Chickamauga Creek in 1864. But Union General William Tecumseh Sherman and his troops forced Confederate armies in the Carolinas, Georgia, and Florida to give up the fight. The Confederates surrendered to the Union in 1865.

Georgia became a Union state again in 1870, but it suffered many hardships in the years that followed. Nearly 200 years of growing cotton had used up most of the nutrients in the soil, and plants would no longer grow as well by the end of the 1800s. In the 1920s, the boll weevil, a tiny beetle that feeds on cotton boll plants, destroyed what was left of the cotton crop.

Many Georgians abandoned their farms and moved to cities and towns. Freed slaves left for cities in northern states. Farmers who stayed tried growing peanuts, soybeans, peaches, and onions. They also raised cattle and poultry. On fields where cotton once grew, new products helped agriculture remain a core industry in Georgia.

Confederate artillery

YEAR

1793   Eli Whitney invents the cotton gin, which makes separating cotton from the sticky plant much easier.

EVENT

- 10 -

General Sherman (leaning on cannon) consults with his officers near Atlanta during the Civil War.

Jewels of Georgia

GEORGIA IS THE LARGEST STATE EAST OF THE MISSISSIPPI RIVER. FIVE STATES BORDER GEORGIA. TENNESSEE AND NORTH CAROLINA MAKE UP GEORGIA'S NORTHERN BORDER. SOUTH CAROLINA LIES TO THE EAST. FLORIDA BORDERS GEORGIA ON THE SOUTH, AND ALABAMA IS TO THE WEST.

Georgia has five land regions, which are referred to as provinces. The Coastal Plain Province makes up the southern half of Georgia. It is named for the 100 miles (161 km) of coastline along the Atlantic Ocean that forms Georgia's southeastern border. The University of Georgia Marine Institute is located on Sapelo Island, just off Georgia's coast. Scientists can study northern right whales and manatees that swim in the surrounding waters.

Sapelo Island (above) is located midway on the coast of Georgia and is the state's fourth-largest island.

The rolling hills of the Piedmont Province stretch north of the coastal plains. Rivers and streams wind through this area. Waterfalls and rapids drop to the lower coastal plains. The Blue Ridge Province is northeast of the Piedmont. Brasstown Bald in the Blue Ridge Mountains is the highest mountain in Georgia. It rises 4,784 feet (1,458 m) above sea level. Amicalola Falls is the tallest waterfall of its kind east of the Mississippi River. It crashes down 729 feet (222 m).

American alligators live in swampy areas of the southeastern U.S. such as Georgia's coastal plains.

The Ridge and Valley Province makes up northwestern Georgia. The tallest ridges in the region are Taylor Ridge and Pigeon Mountain. The Chickamauga Valley, Great Valley, and Rome Valley are lowlands in the province.

YEAR

1821 Cherokee scholar Sequoyah creates the Cherokee alphabet by giving symbols to 86 sounds made in Cherokee speech.

EVENT

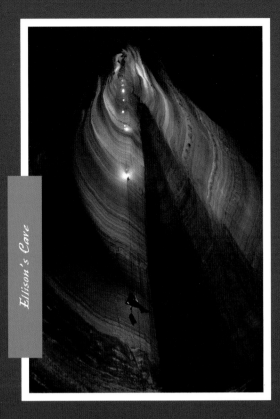

T he Cumberland Plateau is a small area of mountains in the far northwestern corner of Georgia. Sand Mountain is a long, flat-topped mountain at the eastern edge of the plateau. It stands 1,500 feet (460 m) high. Nearby are Lookout and Pigeon mountains. Pigeon Mountain contains the deepest cave east of the Mississippi River, Ellison's Cave. People who like to explore caves go to Ellison's Cave and free-fall down its deep, 586-foot (179 m) pit.

Most of the lakes in Georgia are man-made. Utility companies created some of the lakes to generate power. The U.S. Army Corps of Engineers also dammed rivers and lakes in an effort to control flooding. Still others were developed to

While the deepest cave drop in the U.S. (above) attracts thrill-seekers, people who want outdoor adventure can explore the Blue Ridge Mountains (opposite).

The Chattahoochee River runs through a national forest of the same name in northern Georgia.

supply fresh water or recreation areas. Lake Sidney Lanier, on the upper Chattahoochee, covers 72 square miles (186 sq km) and is the state's largest lake. It was created in the 1950s.

White-tailed deer, hawks, and turkey vultures are found throughout the state. Black bears, alligators, and water moccasin snakes make their homes in the Okefenokee Swamp. Georgia's freshwater rivers and lakes contain many bass, trout, and catfish. Bobcats are common in wooded rural areas, while forests provide habitat for foxes, flying squirrels, and raccoons.

Almost two-thirds of Georgia's land is covered by forests. Forestry is one of Georgia's largest industries. Timber is used in construction products and furniture. Wood is also used to make paper. Other products made from wood include cardboard and chemicals such as turpentine.

The weather in Georgia is mild in the winter. Temperatures in the southern part of the state rarely drop below 50 °F (10 °C), but snow is common in the mountains of northern Georgia. Summers in Georgia are hot and humid, with an average temperature of 88 °F (31 °C). Georgia receives up to 50 inches (127 cm) of rain each year. Hurricanes, tornadoes, and tropical storms often develop in southern Georgia near the Atlantic coast.

Georgia's gray foxes are protected in such areas as the Okefenokee National Wildlife Reserve.

YEAR

1861 Georgia withdraws from the Union and joins the Confederate States.

EVENT

Proud People

SETTLERS FROM MANY COUNTRIES CAME TO GEORGIA
AFTER HERNANDO DE SOTO EXPLORED IT. THEY SAILED THE
ATLANTIC OCEAN FROM SCOTLAND, IRELAND, ENGLAND,
AND GERMANY. SLAVES CAME FROM WEST AFRICA.

The Cherokee tribes in northern Georgia adopted many aspects of the new white culture. They wore European clothes. They built homes and farms that looked like those of white settlers. In 1821, a Cherokee scholar named Sequoyah developed the first Cherokee alphabet. Indians were taught how to read and write. They wrote up their own constitution similar to the U.S. Constitution. They also started their own newspaper, the *Cherokee Phoenix*.

The Georgia gold rush began in 1829. Thousands of white people moved to northern Georgia, hoping to get rich. They wanted to own the land where gold was found, so in the

Although Sequoyah was not a Georgia Cherokee, his work influenced the entire Cherokee nation.

The town of Dahlonega was built by those who rushed to find gold in the nearby mountains.

YEAR
1870   Georgia is readmitted to the Union.
EVENT

- *19* -

Margaret Mitchell's book Gone with the Wind *was made into a popular movie in 1939.*

winter of 1838, U.S. troops forced more than 15,000 Cherokee from their homes. About 4,000 died on the way to Indian Territory in Oklahoma. The route they took is called the "Trail of Tears."

All slaves were freed by the end of the Civil War. But African Americans were not treated fairly for more than 100 years. The Civil Rights movement of the 1950s and 1960s helped bring equal rights to all American citizens. Atlanta-born Martin Luther King Jr. was an important spokesperson for civil rights. Trained as a Baptist minister, King used his persuasive speaking skills to get Americans' attention about inequality among the races. He was assassinated in 1968.

Many other great people have called Georgia home. Baseball legend Jackie Robinson was born in Cairo, Georgia. He was the first black player to sign a contract with a major-league team. He played for the Brooklyn Dodgers in New York for nine years. The team won the World Series six times with Robinson at second base. Author Margaret Mitchell, from Atlanta, wrote the Pulitzer Prize-winning novel *Gone with the Wind*, about the Civil War. It was published in 1936. Jimmy Carter was born in the town of Plains. He became the 39th president of the U.S. in 1977.

The largest share of Georgia's farm income is from ranchers who raise cattle and chickens. Farmers in Georgia produce more chickens that are bred for their meat than any

YEAR

1886   Pharmacist John Pemberton invents the secret recipe for Coca-Cola.

EVENT

YEAR

1926   The first flight into Atlanta's first airport, Candler Field, is a mail plane from Jacksonville, Florida.

EVENT

Although Georgia is no longer the largest peach producer in the U.S., it is still known for its fruit.

other state. Georgia farms produce more peanuts and pecans, too. Food processing is another large industry in Georgia. Food processors make new foods such as peanut butter out of peanuts. Other important industries in Georgia include wood products and automobiles.

Several large businesses are based in Georgia. John Pemberton, a pharmacist from Atlanta, invented Coca-Cola in 1886, and the company's headquarters have been there ever since. The Home Depot also has its main offices in Atlanta. Ted Turner, an Atlanta businessman, runs Turner Broadcasting System (TBS) and Cable News Network (CNN) from Atlanta.

People come to Georgia for many reasons. Some move for better job opportunities. Others enjoy vacationing in Georgia's varied recreational areas. Many people from Florida retire in or own summer homes in Georgia. In the 1970s, many people left the Indochina countries of Vietnam, Cambodia, and Laos to live in Georgia. Recently, high numbers of people from Somalia, Ethiopia, and Russia have made Georgia their new home.

YEAR
1945 President Franklin D. Roosevelt dies at the Little White House in Warm Springs.
EVENT

Jimmy Carter accepted the 2002 Nobel Peace Prize from his hometown of Plains, about 160 miles (258 km) south of Atlanta (opposite).

Just in Georgia

Visitors to Georgia can tour the farm where former president Jimmy Carter grew up in Plains. Then they can visit the Carter Presidential Center in Atlanta. It includes a room that looks like the Oval Office in the White House in Washington, D.C.

A Girl Scout pledges to do her best to serve her community and to obey certain rules.

In Warm Springs, people can find the Little White House. It was built by former president Franklin D. Roosevelt (sometimes called FDR) when he was the governor of New York. He swam in the warm spring waters nearby, hoping that the waters would heal his paralyzed legs. Roosevelt died there in 1945 while posing for a painting. The house today looks much the same as it did when he lived there.

Juliette Gordon Low, who founded the first Girl Scout troop in the U.S., was born in Savannah. Many Girl Scouts from across the U.S. tour her birthplace every year. They participate in hands-on fashion, art, and textiles activities there.

Memories of the 1829 Georgia gold rush are captured in a museum in the northern Georgia town of Dahlonega. Equipment used in the mines and gold nuggets are on display in a museum. Visitors can take an underground mine tour. They can pan for gold and even keep what they find.

The Etowah Indian Mounds near Cartersville is the site where the earliest people in Georgia lived more than 4,000 years ago. One mound covers about three acres (1.2 ha). It is one of the largest mounds in the U.S. Visitors can see parts of the original village and tour a museum there as well.

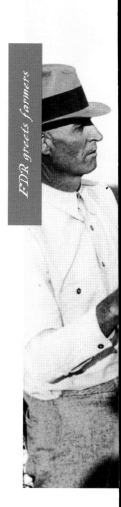

FDR greets farmers

In Warm Springs, Franklin D. Roosevelt came into contact with his hardworking farming neighbors.

Georgia native Martin Luther King Jr. presents his "I Have a Dream" speech in Washington, D.C.

Ray Charles, who went blind at age seven, was known for performing with his signature sunglasses.

Georgia, which is sometimes called the "Empire State of the South," has its own castle. In 1904, furniture businessman Amos Rhodes built a mansion on Peachtree Street in Atlanta with granite from nearby Stone Mountain. Many people get married at the impressive castle.

Atlanta hosted the 1996 Summer Olympics, when more than 10,000 athletes from 197 countries competed in 26 sports. Atlanta's Georgia Dome also hosted Super Bowl games in 1994 and 2000. Atlanta's professional football team is called the Falcons, and the Braves play major league baseball. Two other professional sports teams in Atlanta are the Thrashers of the National Hockey League (NHL) and the Hawks of the National Basketball Association (NBA). The famous Masters invitational golf tournament is held at the Augusta National Golf Course every April.

The American 4 x 400 relay team won the gold medal at Atlanta's 1996 Summer Olympics.

Ray Charles was a famous African American singer who was born in Albany. He recorded the song "Georgia on My

YEAR

1971   Jimmy Carter is inaugurated as Georgia's 76th governor.

EVENT

- *28* -

1996 | The Olympic Stadium in Atlanta hosts the Summer Olympics.

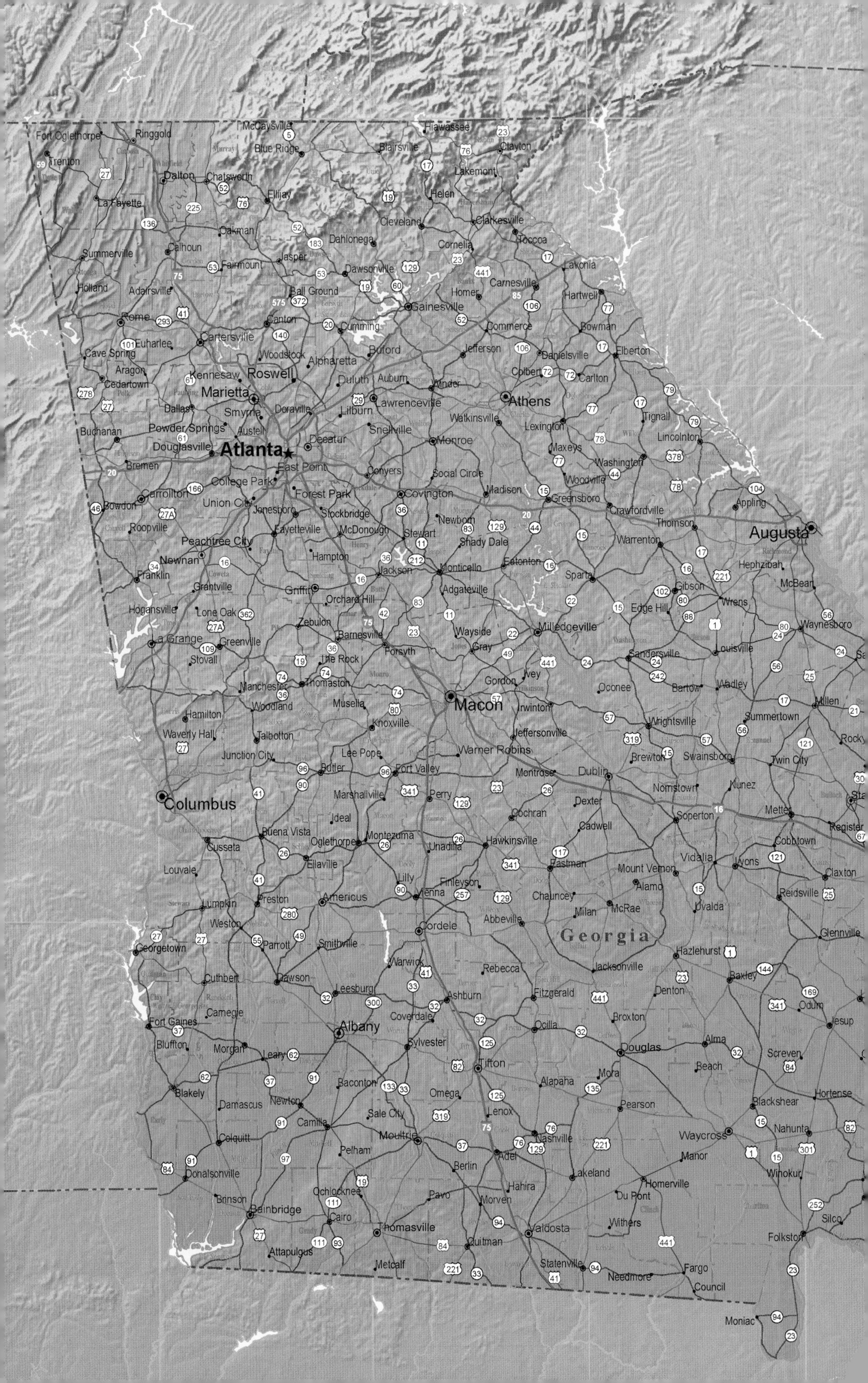
Georgia
Fort Oglethorpe
Ringgold
McCaysville
Hiawassee
Clayton
Trenton
Blue Ridge
Blairsville
Dalton
Chatsworth
Lakemont
La Fayette
Ellijay
Helen
Oakman
Cleveland
Clarkesville
Summerville
Calhoun
Dahlonega
Toccoa
Cornelia
Jasper
Fairmount
Dawsonville
Lavonia
Holland
Adairsville
Ball Ground
Homer
Carnesville
Hartwell
Gainesville
Rome
Canton
Cumming
Commerce
Bowman
Euharlee
Cartersville
Buford
Jefferson
Danielsville
Elberton
Cave Spring
Woodstock
Alpharetta
Aragon
Cedartown
Kennesaw
Roswell
Duluth
Auburn
Winder
Colbert
Carlton
Marietta
Lawrenceville
Athens
Dallas
Smyrna
Doraville
Lilburn
Watkinsville
Tignall
Buchanan
Powder Springs
Austell
Snellville
Lexington
Lincolnton
Douglasville
Atlanta
Decatur
Monroe
Maxeys
Bremen
East Point
Washington
College Park
Conyers
Social Circle
Woodville
Carrollton
Forest Park
Madison
Greensboro
Appling
Union City
Jonesboro
Covington
Crawfordville
Bowdon
Stockbridge
Thomson
Augusta
Roopville
Fayetteville
McDonough
Newborn
Stewart
Shady Dale
Warrenton
Peachtree City
Hampton
Newnan
Jackson
Monticello
Eatonton
Sparta
Hephzibah
Franklin
Grantville
Griffin
Adgateville
Gibson
McBean
Orchard Hill
Edge Hill
Wrens
Hogansville
Lone Oak
Zebulon
Milledgeville
Waynesboro
Wayside
La Grange
Greenville
Barnesville
Forsyth
Gray
Louisville
Stovall
The Rock
Sandersville
Manchester
Thomaston
Ivey
Gordon
Bartow
Wadley
Oconee
Woodland
Musella
Macon
Irwinton
Millen
Hamilton
Knoxville
Wrightsville
Summertown
Waverly Hall
Talbotton
Jeffersonville
Junction City
Lee Pope
Warner Robins
Brewton
Swainsboro
Twin City
Butler
Fort Valley
Montrose
Dublin
Nunez
Norristown
Columbus
Marshallville
Perry
Dexter
Metter
Ideal
Cochran
Soperton
Register
Buena Vista
Montezuma
Cadwell
Cusseta
Oglethorpe
Unadilla
Hawkinsville
Cobbtown
Ellaville
Eastman
Vidalia
Lyons
Louvale
Lilly
Finleyson
Mount Vernon
Alamo
Claxton
Americus
Vienna
Chauncey
Reidsville
Lumpkin
Preston
Milan
McRae
Uvalda
Weston
Cordele
Abbeville
Glennville
Parrott
Smithville
Georgetown
Hazlehurst
Warwick
Rebecca
Jacksonville
Baxley
Cuthbert
Dawson
Leesburg
Fitzgerald
Denton
Ashburn
Odum
Carnegie
Coverdale
Broxton
Fort Gaines
Albany
Ocilla
Jesup
Alma
Sylvester
Bluffton
Morgan
Leary
Tifton
Douglas
Screven
Beach
Mora
Baconton
Alapaha
Blakely
Omega
Hortense
Pearson
Blackshear
Damascus
Newton
Camilla
Sale City
Lenox
Nahunta
Waycross
Colquitt
Moultrie
Nashville
Pelham
Manor
Donalsonville
Berlin
Adel
Winokur
Lakeland
Hahira
Homerville
Ochlocknee
Brinson
Du Pont
Pavo
Morven
Bainbridge
Cairo
Withers
Silco
Thomasville
Valdosta
Folkston
Quitman
Attapulgus
Metcalf
Statenville
Fargo
Needmore
Council
Moniac

QUICK FACTS

Population: 9,363,941

Largest city: Atlanta (pop. 423,019)

Capital: Atlanta

Entered the union: January 2, 1788

Nickname: Empire State of the South

State flower: Cherokee rose

State bird: brown thrasher

Size: 59,425 sq mi (153,910 sq km)—24th-biggest in U.S.

Major industries: agriculture, food processing, wood products

Mind" in 1960. On March 7, 1979, Charles performed the song before the Georgia legislature. One month later, the state declared it Georgia's official state song.

The Pan African Festival of Georgia takes place every spring in Macon. African American, African, and Caribbean people honor their cultures and share traditions with others. The sounds of drumming, jazz, and gospel music are heard throughout the weeklong festival. People enjoy storytelling, dance, and theater events, along with sampling foods from around the world.

Natural wonders and historic places are around every bend in Georgia. Festivals teach visitors and native Georgians about different cultures and remind them of America's past. Georgia's strong agricultural base and many industries keep its economy growing. Whether working, playing, or learning, there is something for everyone in Georgia.

YEAR

2007 Wildfires in southeastern Georgia and Florida burn about 300 square miles (777 sq km) of land.

EVENT

BIBLIOGRAPHY

Bockenhauer, Mark H., and Stephen F. Cunha. *National Geographic: Our Fifty States.* Washington: National Geographic, 2004.

Georgia Department of Economic Development. "Georgia Culture." http://www.georgia.org/Culture.

Georgia Humanities Council. "Slavery in Antebellum Georgia." The New Georgia Encyclopedia. http://www.georgiaencyclopedia.org/nge/Article.jsp?id=h-1019.

Kummer, Patricia. *Georgia.* Mankato, Minn.: Bridgestone Books, 1997.

Marshall, Richard, et al. *Explore America.* Washington, D.C.: AAA Publishing, 1996.

Zenfell, Martha. *Insight Guide United States: On the Road.* Long Island City, N.Y.: Langenscheidt Publishing Group, 2001.

INDEX